Summary: The Japanese Lover By Isabel Allende

: This is a quick read summary based on the novel "The Japanese Lover" by Isabel Allende

NOTE TO READERS:

This is a Summary & Analysis of The Japanese Lover by Isabel Allende. You are encouraged to buy the full version.

Copyright 2015 **by** ABookADay. All rights reserved worldwide. No part of this publication may be reproduced or transmitted in any form without the prior written consent of the publisher.

TABLE OF CONTENTS

Introduction

Setting

Plot Analysis

How to Use This Summary

Part One

Chapter One – Lark House

Chapter Two – Frenchie

Chapter Three – Alma Belasco

Chapter Four – The Invisible Man

Chapter Five – The Polish Girl

Chapter Six – Alma, Nathaniel and Ichimei

Chapter Seven – Irina Bazili

Chapter Eight – Seth Belasco

Chapter Nine – The Fukuda Family

Chapter Ten – The Yellow Peril

Chapter Eleven – Irina, Alma, and Lenny

Chapter Twelve – The Prisoners

Chapter Thirteen – Arizona

Chapter Fourteen – Boston

Chapter Fifteen – The Resurrection

Chapter Sixteen – The Sword of the Fukudas

Chapter Seventeen – Love

Chapter Eighteen – Traces of the Past

Chapter Nineteen – Light and Shadow

Chapter Twenty – Agent Wilkins

Chapter Twenty-One – Secrets

Chapter Twenty-Two – The Confession

Chapter Twenty-Three – Tijuana

Chapter Twenty-Four – Best Friends

Chapter Twenty-Five – Autumn

Chapter Twenty-Six – Gardenias

Chapter Twenty-Seven – The Child Never Born

Chapter Twenty-Eight – The Patriarch

Chapter Twenty-Nine – Samuel Mendel

Chapter Thirty – Nathaniel

Chapter Thirty-One – The Japanese Lover

Part Two

Real World Truths

Thought-Provoking Moments

Prequels/Sequels

Final Analysis

INTRODUCTION

On its surface, the main plot of *The Japanese Lover* is a sweeping tale of clandestine romance set in the midst of social and political upheaval. However, if you peer deeper into the intricacies of the plot, you will notice that at its heart, this is a book about how lives are shaped by both uncontrollable circumstances and by our own actions. The host of characters that the reader will become intimately acquainted with in this book – sweet Irina with her heartbreaking past, Alma the force of nature, steady Ichimei and so on – represent human diversity at its finest and most complex, and show us how life is a constant negotiation between our fears, our values and our passions. Let this book wash over you as you read – see the images of the different lives before your eyes – and imagine what you yourself might do when faced with the same dilemmas our characters are forced to confront. Only by doing so can you truly appreciate the power and beauty of *The Japanese Lover*.

SETTING

The bulk of the story takes place at the Lark House senior residence community in San Francisco, California, where Irina Bazili works to uncover the mystery that is Alma Belasco. The Lark House accommodates mainly progressive-minded seniors of all different ability levels, and provides them with a myriad of ways to pass the time – painting, yoga, political protests, marijuana and so on.

However the book has many settings and it tends to juxtapose opulence with despair – a scene at the enormous Belasco estate Sea Cliff is quickly followed by a scene of life in Japanese internment camp in the desolate Utah desert. These contrasts serve to highlight the starkly different lives and worlds that the different characters in the book occupy.

PLOT ANALYSIS

The plot of this book oscillates between three main stories, with bits and pieces of other tales woven in when appropriate. The novel's relatively short length prevents this from becoming too tedious or confusing, but it can be somewhat difficult to orient oneself within the timeline. It is also difficult at times to tell whether one character is explaining their story to another, or simply reliving it in their head. Readers should pay close attention to the details describing the time period in which events are taking place, as well as to which characters stories and thoughts are being revealed in a particular chapter.

HOW TO USE THIS SUMMARY

The rest of this summary is divided into two parts. Part One contains a brief character guide and a chapter by chapter breakdown. Each section contains a summarization of the grouping, interspersed with analytical comments. Part One is designed to be read alongside the novel. Therefore, each section only contains spoilers for that chapter, although there may be vague hints about what to look for as you continue to read. Part Two discusses the novel and its themes overall, and is designed to be read <u>after</u> completing the novel. Therefore it will contain spoilers about the book's ending.

Part One

Character Guide

Irina Bazili: A 20-something immigrant from Moldova with a dark past. She is a compassionate carer for the elderly at the Lark House and very attached to Alma.

Alma Belasco: A Jewish immigrant who fled Poland as a little girl during World War II. She is about 80 years old in the present day, and the novel details her life. She is very down to earth and yet also very romantic.

Ichimei Fukudo: A second-generation Japanese man who is closely linked with Alma nearly all his life. He is a skilled gardener and artist.

Nathaniel Belasco: Alma's cousin and eventual husband. He is deceased at the start of the novel. He was always very protective of Alma.

Seth Belasco: Alma's grandson. He is in love with Irina and works with her to document Alma's life.

Lenny Beal: An old friend of Alma and Nathaniel's. He and Nathaniel shared a special relationship.

Isaac Belasco: Alma's father-in-law. A very kind man who dearly loved Alma and Nathaniel.

Lillian Belasco: Alma's aunt and mother-in-law. Devoted to Isaac.

Samuel Mendel: Alma's brother. He fought in the British Royal Airforce and was short down over France, but survived.

Dr. Catherine Hope: A doctor who lives and works at the Lark House. She is unable to walk, and helps other patients manage their pain.

Takao Fukudo: Ichimei's father. First-generation Japanese. A skilled gardener.

Heideko Fukudo: Ichimei's mother. Talented businesswoman and community leader.

Megumi Fekudo: Ichimei's sister. Pursues her dream of becoming a midwife, despite many obstacles.

Larry Belasco: Alma's son and head of the Belasco family at the start of the novel.

Kirsten: Alma's assistant. She has Down's syndrome, but is very capable and Alma loves and supports her.

Chapter One – Lark House

The novel starts by introducing us to Irina Bazili: a 23-year-old Romanian immigrant woman who begins working at the Lark House senior residence community. Irina has an ambiguous past. We learn that she has been on her own since she was 15, she is from Moldova, she regrets having left her grandparents, and she is a self-proclaimed addict of fantasy and science fiction. Hans Voigt, the director of the community, thinks her too young for the job, but agrees to take her on temporarily. Lark House is intended to be affordable living for a diverse group of seniors, but in reality the residents are almost all white and middle class. There is significant diversity in religion and political philosophy.

Irina is hired to make life easier for the second- and third-level residents of Lark House – those that require daily assistance. She is not meant to have much contact with the first-level residents, who live independently, or those in the fourth-level, nicknamed "Paradise," who are quickly approaching the end of their lives. Irina is advised by Lupita Farias, the head of the housecleaning staff who makes regular check-ups on the emotional well-being of the seniors, and Dr. Catherine Hope, the youngest resident of the Lark House at 68 and who is described as "the life and soul of the place."

Irina is fascinated by the progressive spirit of the Lark House residents – some of whom regularly participate in public protesting. She is also very intrigued by one resident, Alma Belasco, whose wealth, regal bearing, and aloof nature sets her apart from the other residents.

Chapter Two – Frenchie

Jacques Devine, nicknamed Frenchie, is a 90-year-old resident at the Lark House who is very flirtatious and popular amongst the ladies. He falls in love often, has several children with three different wives and one mistress, and is rumored to have a lot of money saved up. He becomes enamored with Irina and begins to profess his love for her and give her lavish gifts. Irina is not allowed to accept these gifts, nor does she want them, but she does not want to hurt Frenchie's feelings, or give Voigt cause to fire her. She tries to ask Lupita for help, but Lupita is dismissive of the problem. Irina is very distressed by the situation, but before it can escalate much further, Frenchie unexpectedly dies. His family becomes enraged when they discover that just before his death, he changed his will to make Irina the sole heir to his large fortune. Voigt is very disappointed in Irina and plans to fire her, but she astonishes him by saying that she refuses to accept the money. He, and many of the other residents, are extremely impressed by

Irina's behavior, and she is offered a full-time position with a higher salary.

Irina continues to be a very enigmatic figure – an almost too good to be true figure who may or may not have a sinister past.

Chapter Three – Alma Belasco

Alma becomes intrigued by Irina after the incident with Frenchie, and she asks Irina to be her secretary. Irina hesitates at first, but eventually accepts, provided she can still keep her other two jobs at the Lark House and grooming dogs. Alma is a very aloof employer, but Irina is soon able to interpret her demands and they settle into a comfortable business relationship. Alma fascinates Irina – she is fiercely independent, has few friends or acquaintances, does not care for many material possessions, and is very minimalistic in her appearance and décor. She is well-known for her silk-screening and she makes beautiful scarves, hats, and other clothing items that she sells to raise funds for the Balasco Foundation. The Foundation was established by her father-in-law to create green spaces in at-risk neighborhoods in order to discourage crime and build better communities. Seth Balasco, Alma's favorite grandson, stands to inherit the Belasco Foundation. He visits Alma at the Lark House, where he meets

Irina and becomes enamored with her. He tells her that he is planning to write a saga of the Belasco family and of San Francisco itself. This intrigues Irina, but she does not appear to return Seth's romantic feelings. Alma, who enjoys having Seth come to visit her, agrees to help him with the book. She brings Irina along to the ancestral Belasco residence to sort through old possessions, letters and photographs. Irina is very unlike the women Seth usually dates, and Alma knows that his family would most likely disapprove of him marrying a poor immigrant from an unknown family. However Alma herself likes Irina and thinks that she is smart and a good potential match for Seth – she is a rough diamond who just needs some polishing. Alma begins to instruct Irina in culture and manners.

Chapter Four – The Invisible Man

Irina discovers a photograph of a man in Alma's apartment – one of two photograph she displays at Lark House. Alma will only tell her that his name is Ichimei Fukuda and that he painted the bleak painting she keeps on her wall. Irina suspects that Ichimei and Alma are lovers, and she starts to fantasize about what Ichimei is like in person. Every once in a while, Alma disappears from the Lark house for two or three days at a time, packing an overnight bag with silk nightgowns and returning with hotel receipts. She is always melancholy and anxious leading up to the visits, and then she is very happy for a while after she comes back. Seth becomes concerned about these disappearances, and Alma will not give him a straight answer about where she goes. He convinces Irina that, for Alma's own wellbeing, they should secretly find out where Alma goes.

    Seth tells Irina that Alma's personality underwent a drastic change earlier that year. She abruptly decided to stop working with the Belasco Foundation, handed over nearly all her wealth to her son Larry, and packed up and moved into Lark House. She gave her incredulous family no explanation for her behavior, which greatly alarmed them. Seth tells Irina that he is afraid his grandmother is sick and might somehow harm herself or others. He dismisses Irina's speculation about her having a lover. Seth and Irina believe that the key to solving the mystery must lie in the letters Alma receives regularly – but she refuses to show them who they are from or what they say.

The chapter ends with a letter to Alma from "Ichi." Ichi is thanking Alma for another unforgettable honeymoon in Washington, and asking her about a cherry tree he planted near her home many years ago. He tells her he believes there are spirits of the dead all around them, but that they are not malicious or resentful.

Chapter Five – The Polish Girl

Alma begins to tell Seth and Irina the story of how she met Ichimei. Alma Mendel was a young girl when her parents decided to send away from her native country of Poland. World War II was brewing, and while Alma's parents, the Mendels, did not fear for themselves, they wanted their children out of the country. Alma was distraught when her beloved older brother Samuel left to enlist in the Royal Air Force, and then devastated when she had to leave her parents behind.

She was sent to San Francisco to live with her Uncle, Isaac Belasco, and Aunt, Lillian Belasco, and three cousins. She immediately latched onto her older male cousin, Nathaniel, and he reluctantly took her under his wing and protected her. Isaac Belasco came from a long line of successful lawyers and the family lived in a grand estate called Sea Cliff. Isaac was a very kind and generous man. At first, Alma was despondent all the time, but eventually she realized that crying would not solve anything and she became stoic – a personality trait that would continue the rest of her life. She was also beginning to enjoy life at Sea Cliff, especially with her new friends, Nathanial, and the gardener's son, Ichimei Fukuda.

Ichimei's father, Takao Fukuda, had worked at Sea Cliff for many years and Isaac had great respect for him. Alma became fascinated and enamored with Ichimei, particularly with his extraordinary abilities with plants.

Chapter Six – Alma, Nathaniel and Ichimei

For a year, Alma, Nathaniel and Ichimei were close friends. Then Nathaniel had to start secondary school at an all-boys school, where he was singled out for torment by the other boys. Ichimei and Takao began to teach Nathaniel martial arts, which allowed him to defend himself. Nathaniel became more aloof, and Alma and Ichimei continued their close friendship without him. Nathaniel was bitterly unhappy all throughout school, and at one point he even became suicidal. Alma encouraged him to persevere, but she had her own worries. The war was progressing in Europe and she had received very little news about her parents or her brother Samuel since she left. Isaac tried desperately to get in touch with the Mendels, but rumors about the concentration camps were starting to reach Jews in America, and he feared the worst.

Chapter Seven – Irina Bazili

Over the next three years, Irina continued to work for Alma. She learned more about the Belasco family by looking through old photographs. Her relationship with Alma settled into an aunt/niece style relationship. Despite her age, Alma was determined to remain independent.

We learn more about Dr. Catherine Hope. Catherine was mountain climbing when she had an accident, and lost the use of her legs forever. She recovered with the help of Zen Buddhism and when she moved into the Lark House, she decided to start a free pain clinic to help other residents with their ailments.

We learn that Irina has started to feel very safe and comfortable working at the Lark House. She knows that Seth has feelings for her, and does not plan to return them, but she does not worry too much about it. For the most part she enjoys working with the old people at Lark House and she has a remarkable amount of patience and tenderness with them. She learns a lot from them, and even experiences a spiritual awakening while organizing a religious festival for them. She does not make a lot of money, but she feels rich anyway. She enjoys taking care of other people. However, she also greatly appreciates that Alma is so independent and sure of herself, because it means that Irina gets to let someone take care of her for a change.

Chapter Eight – Seth Belasco

Irina frequently accompanies Alma to her weekly dinners at Sea Cliff with the rest of the Belascos. This encourages Seth to come, since he is still in love with Irina. While the Belasco family obviously care for each other, they often bicker amongst themselves.

Despite the unrequited feelings, Seth and Irina form a close friendship, mainly over their shared curiosity about Alma. Seth continues working on his book about the Belascos with Irina's help. Seth is a lawyer just like his family expects him to be, and while he is not bad, he does not have much passion for the job. Alma greatly enjoys having him around, and she often regales Seth and Irina with elaborate tales about her past and what happened to her parents in Europe. She also begins to tell them about the Fukuda family's internment during World War II, though she does not elaborate further on her relationship with Ichimei.

Chapter Nine – The Fukuda Family

Takao Fukuda had left his family home in Japan when he was a young man because he started following the religious path of Oomoto, which preached pacifism, and he knew he could not become a soldier like his family wanted him to be. His parents were upset with his choice, but still bestowed upon him the Fukuda's ancient samurai sword. However, he never tried to integrate into American culture, finding American's materialism, lack of respect and other traits to be distasteful. He quickly became well-known in California for his skill with agriculture. He married a smart and spirited woman from Japan named Heideko and had four children, with Ichimei being the youngest.

Isaac Belasco and Takao began their business relationship during the Depression, and Isaac loved working with Takao to build up his gardens. They eventually made plans to build a nursery for growing flowers, and Isaac planned to give it to Takao's oldest son when he came of age, since Takao could not own land as a first-generation Japanese immigrant.

After Pearl Harbor, the Japanese living in San Francisco began to face harsh discrimination, hate speech and even violence. Evacuation orders were posted and the Fukuda family realized they would be forced into the internment camps. Isaac asked Takao how he could help, and allowed the Fukuda family to bury their family sword at Sea Cliff so that it would not be confiscated or lost. Ichimei asked Alma to look after his cat, Neko. Alma was distraught when she realized that Ichimei would be leaving, and she could not understand why he had to go.

Chapter Ten – The Yellow Peril

The Fukuda family was transferred first to a hastily constructed shelter in San Bruno, where they had to live in a renovated stable stall. Takao was humiliated by this, but Heideko quickly began making the best of the situation. She urged Takao and others in the group to start forming political leadership. Heideko herself was elected to be a representative, and the community started organizing schools and other services amongst themselves.

Six months later, the Fukuda family was transferred to a more permanent camp in Topaz, a desert region in Utah. The climate was very harsh. Again, the Japanese detainees did their best to make the best of their situation, but eventually life in the camp began to change the community structure of the Japanese people. Families were no longer as tight-knit, the younger generations did not give as much respect to their elders, and it was hard to control the young people.

Ichimei and Alma tried to keep in touch with letters,

but Ichimei's were so heavily censored that Alma could barely understand them. He started drawing beautifully detailed pictures of the camp instead.

The chapter ends with a letter from Ichi to Alma, dated in 1986. He tells her how life in the camp was not all horrible, and that afterward, Japanese people finally began to integrate more fully into American society.

Chapter Eleven – Irina, Alma, and Lenny

Alma and Irina are enjoying a rich lunch together in town. Irina discusses the Lark House's money problems with Alma, who is astonished because she has not had to worry about money matters for so long. She begins telling Irina about her family and their business. She discusses how Larry has taken over the charitable Belasco Foundation. Irina tells her that she is lucky to have so many kind-hearted people in her family.

We learn more of Irina's past here – she grew up desperately poor in Moldova with her grandparents Petruta and Costea, who were withered and broken-bodied from poverty. Her mother, Radmila, had become pregnant with her at 16 from an anonymous Russian soldier. When Irina was eight, her mother left to work as a waitress in another country, but ended up being forced into sexual slavery for several years. Eventually, she was able to escape and move to Texas. In 1999, Irina left her grandparents to join her mother in Texas. Her grandmother died a few months later, and her grandfather took his own life shortly after.

In autumn, a man named Lenny Beal comes to live at Lark House. He is very handsome and young-looking, and he and Alma are apparently old friends who lost touch for many years. Irina and Seth are intrigued and Seth has his investigators look into Lenny's history. He takes Irina out to a fancy restaurant and tells her that Lenny was a dentist who must have known Nathaniel. Then he tells Irina that he found out more about Ichimei – that his family was interned at Topaz in Utah during the war.

Chapter Twelve – The Prisoners

Eventually it became harder for Ichimei to write to Alma. Life in the camps was getting harsher and a lot was happening to the Fukuda family. Ichimei's sister Megumi fell in love with a camp guard, his older brother Charlie decided to enlist in the U.S. army, and his brother James was transferred to a different camp as punishment for rebelling in the Utah camp. James' arrest changed Takao and he increasingly retreated from social life at the camp. In contrast, Heideko blossomed at the camp and took on more and more responsibility and leadership, while still trying to keep her husband from completely succumbing to depression.

Megumi also blossomed: she began studying medicine in earnest, and she conducted a secret love affair with the guard, Boyd Anderson. Meanwhile Ichimei earned a reputation at the camp for his gardening skills.

Chapter Thirteen – Arizona

In 1944, Charles was killed in action. In 1945, the concentration camps began closing, and the Fukuda family were given transportation to Arizona. Heideko took advantage of the opportunity to become an American citizen, but Takao was so bitter towards the United States that he refused. Megumi kept searching for ways to pursue a career and medicine and continued corresponding secretly with Boyd. Ichimei began attending secondary school, and although he was not a very strong student, his principal kept encouraging him and praised him for his talents in botany and art.

The chapter ends with another letter from Ichi to Alma, dated 2005. He describes going to see his old principal again, and expresses regret at not being able to see her that week.

Chapter Fourteen – Boston

At first, the lack of communication from Ichimei greatly upset Alma, but she eventually grew to accept it. She was still unsure about what exactly had happened to her parents and brother, Samuel. Isaac believed they were dead, but could not bring himself to tell that to Alma. She became sullen and aloof when she reached puberty, and Nathaniel is the only person she would allow herself to be close too. She was angry when Nathaniel chose to go all the way to Harvard for school. Ichimei and Nathaniel were the two great loves of her life so far, and she could not bear to lose both of them.

After Alma graduated secondary school, she resisted Lillian's attempts to find her a husband and decided to go to a girl's college in Boston instead. She met Nathaniel there and they were both overjoyed to see the other again. She told him about how Lillian was trying to fix her up, but she was still determined to marry Ichimei, a notion that Nathaniel found foolish.

Alma was greatly looking forward to life in Boston, but soon found that she did not fit in well, she could not keep up in her studies, and she didn't have enough pocket money to live as she was accustomed. Winter was miserable and she was almost ready to give up and go home when she discovered silk-screening. She decided she was going to become an artist and eventually travel the world in search of inspiration for her art. Over the next few years, Alma blossomed in both her art and her social life. She still continued to pine for Ichimei.

Chapter Fifteen — The Resurrection

Just before she graduated, Alma began receiving mysterious calls from a stranger with an accent. She attended a wild party right before her graduation, where she almost succumbed to the drugs and alcohol she had been imbibing recklessly, but she was then rescued by a mysterious figure. It was her brother Samuel.

His plane had been shot down over France during the war. He had survived, but lost most of his memories. He spent the rest of the war with a guerilla resistance group, and afterward he had a child with a Hungarian woman. Samuel does not remember Alma himself, but was able to find out who he was by looking at family records. He tells her that his son needs an aunt and asks her to come visit him in Europe. Then he leaves.

Chapter Sixteen – The Sword of the Fukudas

Right before Takao Fukuda died of cancer, he requested to have his Oomoto spiritual leader from California flown out to Arizona. She comes and comforts him as he dies.

When Alma returned home to San Francisco, she believes it will only be for a short time because she plans to move to New York City. Isaac had suffered a heart attack and was left severely weakened, though Lillian tried everything she could to make him feel better. He was overjoyed to see Alma again, because he secretly loved her more than his own daughters. We learn here that Alma was the one who had the idea for the Belasco Foundation, and its charitable work building gardens in at-risk communities.

Alma is thrilled to learn that Ichimei has contacted Isaac and arranged to come for a visit. She greets Ichimei with a hug and a kiss on the mouth, which shocks him. Ichimei had come to ask Isaac if he still has the Fukuda sword buried at Sea Cliff. Isaac tells Ichimei that he wants him to continue the business plan that he and Takao started together – to build the nursery and start growing flowers. Heideko, Megumi and Ichimei immediately move back to San Francisco and throw themselves wholeheartedly into the business, and within a couple years have become successful. Meanwhile, Megumi began studying to be a midwife.

The chapter ends with a letter from Ichi to Alma, dated in 2005, describing how Megumi has unexpectedly decided to retire, something he never thought she would do.

Chapter Seventeen – Love

Alma and Ichimei begin meeting in secret, almost every night in a seedy motel. Alma knows that as progressive as he is, Isaac would never approve of their relationship. Nathaniel knows about it and does not approve, but does not try to stop Alma either.

Ichimei and Alma discover an extraordinary passion and love in each other. When they are together, they forget all about the outside world. "The need for her to know she was loved is insatiable."

Chapter Eighteen – Traces of the Past

Lenny and Alma settle into an easy friendship at the Lark House. Irina feels upset that Alma no longer needs her as much, though Seth reassures that that Alma still wants her around. One day, Irina overhears a conversation between Lenny and Alma while she is washing Lenny's dog nearby. Alma explains to Lenny about giving up her fortune and life at Sea Cliff to move into Lark House, and how it shocked and dismayed the rest of her family. She tells Lenny that she enjoys life at the Lark House and that she is happy because she has love in her life. She tells Lenny about her affair with Ichimei, and he asks her why she married Nathaniel if she loved Ichimei so much. Alma says it was because Nathaniel protected her and she needed that protection. She tells Lenny that her affair with Ichimei is discreet because he has his own wife and children. She reveals that she would never have had the courage to marry Ichimei and live through the prejudice they would have faced.

Lenny and Alma then discuss their relationship, and how they lost touch for so many years. Lenny reveals that he has an inoperable brain tumor and only has six months to live. He plans to live at Lark House until the pain gets too bad and then to end his own life – not an uncommon think at the Lark House. They discuss life after death, with Lenny believes that after death is the same as before birth, and Alma thinking that the spirit does live on and that she hopes she will reconnect with Nathaniel after she dies. Lenny asks Alma if she will help him die when the time comes.

In a letter dated 2002, Ichi discusses growing older, suggesting that it is not something to fear, but a natural thing.

Chapter Nineteen – Light and Shadow

Alma enjoys helping Seth with his book because it allows her to reconstruct her past, and to process everything that has happened to her over the course of her life. She edits some of her memories, and she never discusses Ichimei. Irina is always there to assist her.

Alma realizes that her body is finally starting to deteriorate, which scares and irritates her though she tries her best to accept it.

A collection of photographs Nathaniel took of Alma get put on display in a gallery in San Francisco, and Seth and Irina convince Alma to go look at them. Irina is entranced by the photographs, some of which show Alma naked, and amazed at how Nathaniel was to capture such beauty and complexity with a picture.

One day, while at the theater, Alma experiences severe chest pains. She goes to the hospital and the next day, for the first time ever, Alma spends the day in bed. Over the next couple weeks, Alma realizes that her body and mind are deteriorating faster than she thought they would. She begins to think about death more and more often. She speaks about Nathaniel to Irina, referring to him as her guardian angel. She discusses Nathaniel's protectiveness of her and wishes she could have been a better wife to him. Irina insist that

Nathaniel must have felt fortunate to have her.

Chapter Twenty – Agent Wilkins

In October, FBI agent Roy Wilkins comes to Lark House looking for Irina. Irina is surprised but not upset to see him, and at first they talk to each other like old friends. Then Wilkins calls her Elisabeta and Irina tells him to remember that is not her name anymore. He asks her if she is in therapy, and when the conversation starts to upset her, he pulls her in for a hug.

The Wilkins begins discussing a crime that was committed against Irina. We do not know at this point what that crime was, but Wilkins tells Irina that she is entitled to compensation from the perpetrators. Irina insists that she does not want to seek compensation, or ever have to face the perpetrators again. He gives her his card in case she changes her mind. Irina is horrified at the thought that the people in her life will discover what that was all about.

That night, Cathy calls Irina in to speak to her and asks her about Wilkins. Irina tries to resist telling her anything, but

Cathy persists, telling Irina that it will do her good to get it off her chest.

Now we learn about Irina's past. Her mother Radmila saved up money so Irina could join her and her new husband in Texas. Irina said good-bye to her grandparents and traveled to Dallas all by herself. There she met her mother and her new stepfather, Jim Robyns. Robyns and Radmila both worked hard, but they also drank hard and took drugs. Irina lived with them for two years, forced to obey certain rules her stepfather laid out, until one day Agent Wilkins knocked on the door.

Chapter Twenty-One – Secrets

One night, after one of Alma's disappearances, Seth invites Irina to go get sushi and discuss Alma. They speculate more about Ichimei. Seth tells Alma he asked his father, who remembers Ichimei came to the house to build another garden onto the estate at Sea Cliff. Seth tells Irina that Larry told him Ichimei had an aura – a visible aura like a halo that could be seen in certain lights – and that Ichimei could make his hands hot or cold as if by magic. Irina is skeptical, but Seth tells her Larry is such a skeptical person that if he said it, it must be true. Larry also told Seth that Ichimei visited Alma for several years, then disappeared for a while.

Irina and Seth speculate about when Ichimei and Alma might have been lovers and if Nathaniel ever knew. Seth once again professes his love for Irina.

There is another letter from Ichi to Alma, dated in 2004. Ichi talks about the samurai sword that was buried at Sea Cliff.

Seth drinks too much saki at the restaurant and Irina has to take him back to her place because he cannot drive. She is ashamed to let him see the rundown house where she lives in a makeshift apartment. Irina confesses that she suffers from nightmares often. She has a hard time falling asleep that night, and in the morning Seth is gone, but she has a terrible headache.

Chapter Twenty-Two – The Confession

The next day Seth shows up and apologizes for his behavior. Irina asks him to take her and Alma's cat, Neko, who is sick, to the vet. The vet says Neko needs an operation which Seth pays for. Afterward, he carefully asks Irina to move out of her filthy, decrepit apartment and move in with him, to help him finish his book. Irina tells him he will get bored with her and throw her out eventually and then she will have nowhere to go. Seth tells her that he wants to marry her. Irina starts to cry – Seth's love is the stuff of fairy tales, but she is not able to love him back. She tries to convince him that if he knew her past he wouldn't want her, but Seth insists that is not true. He asks her to at least come see his apartment before she decides.

Seth's home is very elegant, but sparsely decorated and very bare. Irina asks if she can take a bath since she has not been able to take one in years. She luxuriates in the bath for a long time and falls asleep almost immediately after. When she wakes up, Seth gives her sad news – Neko is dying. Irina feels sick so she spends the rest of the night and next day in Seth's apartment. When he comes back home, she tells him they have to talk.

She tells him that for the two years that she lived with her mother and stepfather, her stepfather forced her to take pornographic pictures and raped her. He told her that it was normal, and that if she complied, he would send money to her grandparents. Eventually, FBI Agent Wilkins tracked her down and was able to arrest both her stepfather and mother for allowing it to happen.

Seth tells her that he can protect her from her stepfather forever, but Irina protests and says that the point is that her pictures are still out there on the internet and anyone could find them. His family could never accept her. Seth tells her it doesn't matter. She tells him that she is not sure she can ever be intimate with someone else and he tells her he can take things as slowly as she needs him to.

Chapter Twenty-Three – Tijuana

Alma lies to Ichimei and tells him that she is sterile. However then she becomes pregnant and she panics. She cannot tell Ichimei because she has realized that she cannot marry him – they are from too different worlds and she is not ready to give up being wealthy and upper class. She realizes that if she married Ichimei she might grow to resent him. So instead she tells Nathaniel, who is shocked and angry, but willing to help her. Alma tells him she wants to go to Tijuana to get an abortion, However when they get there, the abortion "clinic" is shoddy, the men are shady, and there is no anesthetic – only tequila. Nathaniel sees the look of panic on Alma's face and tells the men that she has changed her mind.

Alma is deeply ashamed, but she still cannot bring herself to give up her high social class and money to marry Ichimei. She does not even recognize herself as the girl Ichimei loves anymore. She arranges to meet Ichimei early in the motel room. He has been suspicious for some time that something is wrong with Alma. She gives him a carefully rehearsed speech about how they come from different worlds and will never work out, and how she has decided to go to London to continue studying art. Ichimei listens silently and then tells Alma that he understands. He kisses her one last time, walks her to her car, and then leaves without looking back.

    In a letter dated 1969, Ichi explains how he was heartbroken and felt cheated when Alma broke things off, but he grew to understand why she did it.

Chapter Twenty-Four – Best Friends

Alma and Nathaniel get married in a small, private ceremony at Sea Cliff. At first there is a bit of a scandal because they are cousins, but Isaac shuts down any negative talk and gives the couple his blessing. They do not consummate the marriage. Nathaniel tells Alma that he knows she loves Ichimei and she tells him that as soon as the baby is born he is free to divorce her and pursue any woman he wants. He tells her that while he has never thought of her romantically, they can still have a good marriage. They just have to take it one step at a time.

Alma and Nathaniel stay at Sea Cliff, where everyone can see that there is little passion in their marriage. Lillian is concerned about this and tries to get them to be more affectionate, but Alma laughs it off.

Meanwhile, Ichimei has heard of this marriage and has grown gloomy and sullen. His mother and sister cannot understand his attitude. Heideko decides to try and lift her son's spirits by taking him back to Japan so they can visit his relatives. When they get to Japan, she leave Ichimei on his own with very little money. He travels his own path around Japan, walking until his sad memories of Alma wear away.

    In a letter from Ichi to Alma, dated 1994, he explains that while he was wandering through Japan, he learned how to live a life without certainty.

Chapter Twenty-Five – Autumn

Irina is beginning to have to help Alma with certain tasks, such as getting ready in the morning, but neither are willing to admit that she might have to move to the second level of Lark House and star receiving regular care. Alma misses her cat Neko fiercely, since he had to be put down, but she is not willing to get a pet that will outlive her. She values her friendship with Lenny immensely – before she did not even realize how lonely she had become after living a mainly solitary life. Alma spent many years being isolated from the rest of society, and she preferred it that way. She enjoyed the work that the Belasco Foundation did for the poor, but never wanted to mingle with them herself.

Alma had been regularly receiving gardenias in the mail every Monday, and all of a sudden they stop but she gives no indication that she has noticed. She secretly has noticed her body and mind breaking down more and more, to the point where she vaguely hopes every night that she might just slip away into death in her sleep. She thinks about how she lost her fear of death thirty years earlier after watching Nathaniel die. She and Lenny spend a lot of time talking about death and the possibilities of an afterlife. Alma thinks about how none of the therapists or psychologists that Lark House employs could possibly understand how old people think about death.

Alma also makes the very difficult decision to close her painting studio. She would have shut it down before, but she has an assistant, Kirsten, with Down's syndrome, who has difficulty adjusting to new routines. She makes sure that Kirsten will be more than adequately taken care of.

Chapter Twenty-Six – Gardenias

Seth shows up to the Lark House with gardenias for Alma and asks her about Ichimei. She is shocked and angry that he knows anything about Ichimei and he reveals what Irina and he have discovered on their own. Alma is very fond of Irina and believes she will be good for Seth, even if the rest of the Belascos are having a hard time warming up to her.

Alma tells Seth that she has more to tell him and Irina.

Seth summons Irina to Alma's room, giving her an escape from an uncomfortable confrontation between Catherine and Voigt about a client's rights to commit suicide. Alma tells Irina and Seth that she is going to tell them a story of her life from the beginning, but they must swear to keep her secrets until after she is dead. She recounts everything we as readers have learned so far in the story, up until the point where she is pregnant with Ichimei's child and married to Nathaniel. Seth is very shaken and demands to know if he is actually a Fukuda, instead of a Belasco. Alma tells him he is a Belasco.

Chapter Twenty-Seven – The Child Never Born

Isaac and Lillian were thrilled that they would soon have a grandchild named Belasco. They pulled out all the stops to get ready for the baby, and Alma got so swept up in the anticipation that it lessened her grief of having ended things with Ichimei. She and Nathaniel continued to share a very close bond, even if it is as best friends rather than as lovers. She felt wholly protected and safe with him. She told him that he does not have to remain faithful to her, just to be discreet.

Then, one day as they were relaxing in the Belasco's family house in Lake Tahoe, Alma suffered an attack of eclampsia. The baby had to be taken out and at five and half months, had no hope of survival. Nathaniel was the only one to see the child and he wept in grief at the loss of its life.

Seven months later, Nathaniel took Alma on a trip through Europe to cheer her up. They had settled into a friendly, but very celibate routine at Sea Cliff, but while in Europe, Alma begs Nathaniel to sleep with her. Their lovemaking was awkward and fumbling, but they kept doing it. In the meantime, Alma continued to develop her artistic talents and brand.

Nathaniel also told Alma that she was under no obligation to remain faithful to him, but it is then that she told him she is pregnant again. Isaac and Lillian were once again thrilled and get everything ready for the baby. Their son Lawrence, nicknamed Larry, was born healthy and without complications. He spent much more of his young years with his grandparents than with his parents, who live their own separate and very busy lives.

Chapter Twenty-Eight – The Patriarch

Larry's birth rallied Isaac's health for several years and for the first four years of his life, Larry and Isaac were practically inseparable. Then one day Isaac collapses and dies. Later Larry would remember those first four years very clearly as the happiest time of his life. After his death, Lillian suffered from blindness, but she continued to dote on Larry for the rest of her life.

Alma thought often of contacting Ichimei, but could never bring herself to do it. Then, at Isaac's funeral, Ichimei shows up with a new wife, Delphine. Alam was rattled by this, and afterward she waited for Ichimei to get in touch with her, but he never did. Finally she started calling the Fukuda flower shop, but when she did it was always Delphine that would answer and she would hang up. Delphine knew that it was Alma on the phone, however, and eventually a very polite letter from Ichimei arrives. Alma is able to read between the lines of the letter and knows that Ichimei wants her to stop trying to contact him.

For the next seven years, Alma settles into a routine of traveling the world for inspiration for her art. She and Nathaniel continue to be the best of friends and she and Nathaniel take Larry on trips around the world as well. Alma and Nathaniel have fairly chaste relationship, and they both accept that they have their own private worlds and affairs. Alma tries to have love affairs in Europe, but finds no passion in one-night flings. She is never able to forget Ichimei.

The chapter ends with a letter from Ichi to Alma, dated 1978, where Ichi praises the movement Alma has achieved in one of her art pieces.

Chapter Twenty-Nine – Samuel Mendel

Alma met up with her brother Samuel in Paris in 1967, after a long trip spent in Japan studying *sumi-e* painting. Alma and Samuel had become friends over the years through correspondence with letters. For Samuel, it was the first time he has visited Paris since the war. They rented a car and drove to the town where he supposedly died after his plane was shot down, where there was even a memorial placed for him by the Belascos. A young caretaker at the memorial site invited them back to her house, where her grandfather lives, who was part of the Resistance.

Samuel and the French man spent the rest of the evening discussing their experiences during the war. Samuel talked about coming to after his plane went down, making his way to the Resistance forces, spending months cold and hungry, and finally be captured and sent to Auschwitz-Birkenau. Then after the camps were liberated, he went to assist with the creation of the State of Israel.

After that, Alma and Samuel went to Poland to see if they can find any remaining traces of their parents' lives, and after that they visited Auschwitz. Samuel struggled to understand how ordinary people become monsters. He cryptically implied to Alma that he himself had turned into a monster when he was a soldier, but wouldn't give her any more details than that.

Chapter Thirty – Nathaniel

This chapter details the end of Nathaniel's life, describing how a "sly illness" was inside him for years before it started to kill him. He began to exhibit flu-like symptoms at first, but then they did not go away. He was forced to give up his work and his hobbies. Alma became terrified of losing him and threw herself into finding remedies. She gave up her art for a while to concentrate on him.

She also stopped seeing Ichimei – they had reunited and become lovers in the years preceding Nathaniel's illness. They kept their relationship very discreet and secret from their spouses. After Nathaniel fell ill and she had to stop seeing Ichimei for a time, he began sending her flowers and writing her letters.

A letter from Ichi to Alma, dated 1984, expresses sympathy for Alma for dealing with Nathaniel's illness, and expresses his sadness at not being able to see her.

Alma and Nathaniel started sleeping next to each other

again at night, just holding each other when they could not sleep. Eventually Nathaniel says he needs to confess something to Alma. He reveals that he knew from a young age that he was a homosexual, and that he kept his love affairs completely secret from everyone, even her. Then he met Lenny Beal in a Turkish bath in 1976 and the pair quickly became lovers. They rented a studio apartment in San Francisco and met with each other often over the years. Lenny settled down after he met Nathaniel, and blossomed under his influence, eventually becoming a successful dentist. When Nathaniel became sick, he and Lenny tried to continue their relationship as much as possible, but with him being housebound, they were not able to see each other.

  Alma called Lenny up and invited him to the house, thoroughly relieved and glad to be able to get help from someone who loved Nathaniel as much as she did. She told him to consider Sea Cliff as his home, and he and Nathaniel were free to spend the night together. Eventually they discovered that Nathaniel had AIDS, but they told everyone that it was cancer, to avoid outing him. While they tried every remedy available to try and help him, Nathaniel died less than a year later, Lenny and Alma at his side.

Back at the Lark House, Lenny and Alma wonder how they had let their friendship fade after that, when they had shared such an ordeal together. They joke about getting married and find great happiness in their relationship with each other.

Chapter Thirty-One – The Japanese Lover

One morning, Irina goes to see Alma and discovers that her room is empty and her overnight bag is gone. Irina is not alarmed because Alma does this often. However later she receives a call that Alma is in intensive care. She wrecked her car and her legs and organs had been crushed. The doctors say that without extensive surgery there is nothing much that can be done other than keep her comfortable while she slips away.

The Belascos come to visit Alma in the hospital. Irina visits Alma and asks if she would like her to call Ichimei. Instead, Alma asks for Kirsten. She wants to speak to Kirsten alone. Later Irina spends the night in Alma's room, already grieving at the thought of losing the woman who had taught her so much and become so important to her. She wants Alma's suffering to end, but she does not want to lose her. She thinks about all the people she has known in her life, and the grief of losing them, or the joy of still having them in her life.

Then, in the darkest hour of the night, Irina witnesses

Alma receive a visitor. She instantly recognizes him as Ichimei. Ichimei is at Alma's bedside, leaning over her, and she wakes up and says his name. Irina leaves to give them privacy. The next morning she mentions Ichimei to a nurse, who tells her she must be mistaken because there were no visitor for Alma in the night. They go into Alma's room to discover that she has passed away.

    Irina attends Alma's funeral and throws a gardenia onto her body as they lower it into the ground. Unexpectedly, the Belascos invite Irina to sit *shiva* with them for Alma. After the mourning process is over, Irina goes to Lark House to deal with Alma's remaining possessions. She becomes overcome with grief and weeps. Then Kirsten comes to visit. Once Kirsten realizes that Alma is not coming back, she gives Irina a backpack. Irina discovers that it is full of the letters Alma has received from Ichimei over the years. Irina is so overcome with gratitude that Alma loved her so much as to trust her with the letters, that she realizes that her fears – of what her stepfather did to her – are not great enough to stop her from living her life and being happy.

That night, Irina greets Seth with a hug and a kiss and shows him the letters. There are 106 love letters from Ichi in total, dating from 1969 onward. But there are no letters after 2010, which puzzles Irina because Alma had continued to receive letters from Ichimei throughout her time at Lark House. Seth reveals that Ichimei had died shortly before Alma moved to Lark House and that she continued to resend his letters to herself, and to visit the places where they had been lovers – alone. Irina insists that this cannot be true because she is sure she saw Ichimei in the hospital right before Alma died. Seth tells her that she must be mistaken, that she saw what she wanted to see.

Irina says that she believes that Ichimei must have come back for Alma – that she loved him so much he came back for her.

The book ends with Ichimei's final letter to Alma, dated 2010. He tells her how much he loves her, how exuberant and boisterous the world is, and that he does not mind being old, because with Alma they are 17 again.

Part Two

Missed Themes/Symbols

Gardens and growing things consistently pop up throughout the book, most commonly associated with Ichimei's green thumb. Ichimei's talent with gardens is actually somewhat contradictory, considering the love for wandering that he tells Alma about in one of his letters. However gardens also serve as a powerful symbol of the diversity of life, and what is required for different beings to survive. Isaac and Takao, and later Ichimei, devote themselves to bringing plants in from other areas of the world and figuring out how to make them thrive in San Francisco. This is especially poignant when you consider that Isaac was the descendent of immigrants, and Takao was practically fresh off the boat, as was Alma at the time, and all three managed to make their way in life in very different ways.

REAL WORLD TRUTHS

The Japanese Lover deals with several social, political and moral topics in an unflinching manner. Irina's horrific abuse at the hands of her stepfather is a tragic reality in the lives of children all over the world, as is the abuse her mother suffered as a sexual slave in Europe. The book also discusses how something like that lives forever in today's world, when nothing can truly be erased from the Internet. The idea of putting your past behind you and being able to truly move on without it coming back to haunt you is not something that Irina will ever truly be able to do.

The book also takes a look at one of the blackest marks in the book for the United States – the internment of thousands of innocent Japanese immigrants and Japanese-Americans. The fact that it happened in a country that professes to defend freedom for all is a bleak reminder that freedom must constantly be fought for.

THOUGHT-PROVOKING MOMENTS

Death and the possibility of an afterlife are discussed throughout the book. Lenny and Alma have a particularly interesting discussion about it in chapter eighteen, when Lenny seems to think that after death is just like before birth, but Alma seems to believe that after death it will be possible to see her loved ones again. Irina also wrestles with this topic, as she begins to believe during her time at Lark House that her grandparents are watching over her. She also believes at the end of the novel that she has been granted a glimpse of the afterlife, when she sees Ichimei come for Alma on her deathbed.

This is always a thought-provoking topic because it is a mystery that can never truly be solved. It also begs the question of how to provide counseling or therapy to elderly individuals who have such fundamentally different ideas of what will happen to them once they pass on.

PREQUELS/SEQUELS

There is no room for a prequel to the story, but it is certainly left wide open for a sequel detailing Irina and Seth's relationship. When the story ends, she is struggling to find out whether or not she will ever be able to trust him with physical love, after the horrific abuse that her stepfather inflicted on her. A sequel could explore her healing process. The Belasco family is also not entirely thrilled at the idea of accepting a poor, non-Jewish, immigrant girl into their family, so that would provide a sequel with some of the same social and moral quandaries that made *The Japanese Lover* so complex.

FINAL ANALYSIS

The Japanese Lover crams so much into its pages that readers will be thinking about the different aspects of this novel long after they have put it down. It's at once a gripping, heart-breaking romance as well as a down-to-earth look at the possibilities and impossibilities of following one's heart at the expense of all else. And while it may veer into overly soppy territory once in a while, *The Japanese Lover* manages to portray life, and the people in it, at their best, at their worst, and at all the stages in between. This is a powerful book.

Made in the USA
Coppell, TX
22 July 2023